The Ladies and Gentlemen
of the Dead

Dominic Fisher

THE
BLUE
NIB

The Ladies and Gentlemen
of the Dead

Dominic Fisher

Edited by: Shirley Bell

ISBN   978-1-9993655-2-3

For Chris and Robin

Thanks and acknowledgements:

Poems in this collection have been previously published in *Brittle Star, Hailing Foxes* (Gert Macky Press), *Magma, Poetry Ireland Review, Poetry Salzburg Review, Raceme, Salt in the Wind* (Elephantsfootprint), *South Bank Poetry,* and *The Interpreter's House.* A version of *Firming the soil* was broadcast in *How to Write a Poem* (BBC Radio 4 with Glyn Maxwell 2016), and *Hardware visitations* won the Bristol Poetry Prize 2018.

With thanks to Shirley Bell at *The Blue Nib*, Cathy Fisher for the cover art, the Friday morning poetry group, Colin Brown and Deborah Harvey at The Leaping Word poetry consultancy, and to Chris Lindop.

Contents

ALLOTMENTS

A fox's late winter blessing

May soil go soft beneath your claws
to give you beetles grubs and worms
the alleyways be full of food, the roots
and stones conspire to keep you dry.

May your nose know all the languages
of dead and living. May everything
by its nose learn your range and kin
your songs shake sleepers from their dreams.

May cats and dogs who think they're hard
see your teeth and think again.
May seagulls never get there first
and wires and highways not restrain you.

On long green evenings or belated dawns
may your own kits play on and on,
moon after moon, and even after
this city itself has gone.

Thinker

My friend the crow
is a thinker. So
pigeons do well on the cabbages
and the green redcurrants
but the crow can stab a slow-worm
through hot black plastic.

In the broken light
and slantwise rain
this liquid piece of night
my friend the crow, picks
a moment, eyes the pigeons
snaps up their chicks.

Just don't
anthropomorphise me though.
I'm not like that, she says
my friend the crow.

Grasshopper

Motionless on the rippling sheet of green
ginger and shiny, all joints and feelers

the small grasshopper on a pumpkin leaf
is a grasshopper on a pumpkin leaf.

It engages in no tedious talk
on work with any moralising ant.

As you celebrate this obvious truth
your attention wavers for a moment.

You catch a faint click like a camera.
The grasshopper is nowhere to be seen.

Blackbird in a tank

Now inlet and outlet make no difference.
The tank came out of a loft years ago

and became the dull box for catching rain
where we wash the mud off our spades and forks.

I smelt it before I saw the blackbird
half submerged among leaves in a corner.

Sodden though it was it flew one more time
eyes shut, off a fork, into the brambles.

It had been an upside down tree in there
the sky in the water, the hidden bird.

Digging

The first row begins like all the others.
Spade by spade, day by day, the first row's dug.

The next bed begins in just the same way
with the first spade in the first row again.

Our third bed, half dug now, will be broad beans.
Turned earth and hard ground alike are marked out.

Subsequent beds haven't been plotted yet
though there's a rough plan for the next season.

Sometimes you dig things up: a smooth white stone
a button, row by row and year by year.

Putting the work in

Twenty-odd plots run side by side downhill
to brambles, nettles, and a padlocked gate.

To get one you need to be on the list
and you can lose it, because there are rules.

They're mostly about putting the work in
not letting couch and thistles take over.

It's also true that you can over-extend
a metaphor, make too much work of it.

The long hills beyond town fade towards grey
or climb on beneath the vapour trails.

Magpie finishes the job

Flash bastard, too late to stop you
doing a flit now with the gold
slow-worm and its signal-bright
dab of red in the mid-May air.

Or maybe it was only the tail you got.
So not so nifty after all. But the bit
convulsing on the grass confirms
you had the meatier part.

Scant consolation, the leftovers,
to the mate with the brood of two
or three chocolate striped shoelaces
all deep down in a crack suddenly.

And clever clever bleeder, coming back
all slick black-and-white rainbow.
Just walk in, quick jab, up with the gold
stump too in the mid-May air.

Lasius niger

Like Godzilla in a hat
your shadow falls across black ants.

Silently (or maybe not) they scuttle
up and down the face the spade has cut

hurry eggs through smashed up suburbs
in Aleppo, Tokyo, Ancient Rome.

Afternoon traffic, sirens, aircraft
go all but unnoticed as you watch

the opened labyrinths, the sticky clay.
You raise your hat. Godzilla waves.

Firming the soil

i.m. RH

It's just as well that you're not here today
you wouldn't see the point in clearing weeds.
I'll see you in the pub I'd hear you say.
Yes, be there soon. I'd go on spacing seeds.
You'd get the drinks in, ask what took so long
so I'd explain about the beans and peas
and you'd concede you wished that you were strong
then we'd discuss the course of your disease.

Remember how we launched our ships for Troy
or was it Barcelona after all?
So were we heroes? What did we destroy?
Now half of what we did I can't recall.
I firm the soil. You went on ahead.
Like Ulysses, I'm questioning the dead.

Sparrow

You don't see her coming behind you
the sparrowhawk, you don't know she is there

till a flurry on open ground before you
and one instant of eye to bright brown eye.

Cheeping sparrow and silent hawk, gone
into the shade, the ivy and elder.

The sparrow that flew long ago through a feast
in a hall, this was swifter than that.

A few feathers blow about in front of you.
You didn't see her coming behind you.

Bee in a poppy

Bee near drowning
in more colour than we see.

Working the crown in your trance
you drench yourself in gold.

Desire is between two poles,
the flower and the hive

but you must also dance
so the tribe can find the flower.

If there is no dancing
we will not survive.

The plot-holder on five

He's out there anyway in November
in some sense always, mid plot and stooped
among his heavy cabbages his pale leeks
while the weather holds for one grey hour.

Winter sun and memory simplify
the picture of white hair stocky frame
the black opening of the shed where everything
is cleaned oiled sharpened lined up and labelled.

All the same he's halfway somewhere in those layers
of soil and sky, the light or dark rotations.

Of course he's there before you, there more often
of course he grows more stuff than almost anyone.
He's there again with his back towards us
the earth as thick as fruit cake at his feet.

The flowers on his beans are firebirds flickering
among their canes and in the shadows of the leaves.
The pea flowers are falling clean as cotton
the pods like fresh tongues are getting long and fat.

He could be a patch of sky in his overalls
out in the wind. He turns, waves, works on.

White field

Every plot is one faint blue-grey
its planting slipping from memory.

Paths have gone from the page
the unexpected snow made

and what's green is wilted or bitter
onions and leeks going under.

What are you here for with slow feet
in this half-sunk lettering?

Go home in your own fading script
through blurred air and the falling day.

Final allotment

I've been working for years
to get this plot
under some sort of control.
I had thought it was my so-called career
(though it proved not)
some distant height, that was the final goal.

But it turns out it was this lot
this weedy ground at my feet
this trodden clay
which is all we've got
this allotment, so to speak
where the work is never complete.

Sometimes you think you see a way.
Other times you start to understand
that all the hardest things are here
stubborn, tangled, close at hand.

When we leave this field

By June the waist-high grass will come to no one's waist
but will be blonde and over-reached by finches in the thistles.

Not far behind, the brambles will be quick and wicked,
keys and wings will drop and root, go tall as sycamore and ash.

Three-inch oaks will shelter in the beetle-green of holly
and jays will scream overhead among the ghosts of bean poles.

And whether the road at the top is heavy with retreat
whether or not there's smoke on the hills behind the motorway

there will be seasons if no festivals, the moon will enter
empty roofs, the tumbled streets will fill with birds at dawn.

What's already setting seed will grow and fall and grow again.
No paradox of knowledge will mar these mangled Edens then.

STEPS

Water paper gold

Keep them from us
        with fences of water
        wider deeper
        colder than they know

Keep them from us
        with bricks of gold
        with visible fences
        and walls of glass

Look how our horizon encircles
no deserts no blinded cities

Look how the sky is divided
into our sky and their sky

We are here
        where our forbears fought for these
                roundabouts and central reservations
                these slip-roads these signs these limits

Where we are
        we speak no ifs or buts
                our own straightforward language

Where they are
        is the Tower of Babel
                an encampment of rubbish
                one pair of jeans and no signal

Some say we should open something some part
that is itself a fence or wall with locks and gates

They say each of us is adrift in a shaky boat
migrating across equal seas the same terrains

They forget
        our long lineage and its claims
                its treaties maps and standards

Keep us in
        with fences of privilege with preference
        with ancestral divisions

Keep us in
        with memories and forgetting
        and our well-fed fears

Withhold from them
        that little we have
        with locks of water paper gold
        with walls they see and we will not

Papaver

'Cultivated and disturbed ground.'
The Natural History Book, Dorling Kindersley, 2010

Even in Blighty the seedpods
go shiny and hard
capped with segmented
vegetable stars
upright and brittle
on the ends of their stalks

then shiver together
faintly hissing
like far-off percussion
cicadas somewhere
or a nearer-by
community of snakes.

But gone to pale wood
and for lack of heat here
these shut cups would be
no good to the middle man
of no interest to
the poisonous helicopters.

Though where sun allowed
each seed inside
if not rattled out
by the wind or chance
but sprinkled as if from
some imperial pepperpot

might then germinate
in broken ground
between Moscow and Kabul
enter bloodstreams in Hong Kong
the outskirts here, any town
across a border.

This one dot
of poppy could
anaesthetise all pain
waste empires, make
our cornfields bleed
or decorate our bread.

Cultivated and disturbed
companion of the nodding gods
Nyx, Hypnos,
Morpheus, Thanatos.
Mauve silk, red spots.
Black heart. Full stop.

Crossing Gaol Ferry Bridge

The afternoon is pulsing blue
and all along the iron railings
the length of the waterfront
there are stalls with coloured glass
leather, twisted wire, DVDs.

Everyone is making claims
on your wallet or your heart
is playing music for your change
by Pero's Bridge, or holding out
a shaking plastic cup.

Someone sits cross-legged
with a dog inside their coat
there on the other side.
Light bounces off the harbour
the last leaves shine like coins.

Same scene on the swing bridge
you give or you don't give.
Either way you deny or hope
a little money could release you
or a fall of gold might fix this.

You come to Gaol Ferry Bridge
where everyone has stopped.
Trucks and vans both ends
like big bright boxes, rear doors
in red and yellow chevrons.

A fire crew is approaching
a bundle on the mudbank
and washing over all of us
        pulsing blue
        pulsing blue.

Llangurig

Driving on up to the snowline, we came
close to a place on a bend where I saw
someone on foot heading into the snow
years ago now, like a pale grey mark
looking for sheep or just lost in himself.

Little has altered. At this height things don't.
Fence-posts and wire need replacing at times
gorse dies and grows at the side of the road.
Maybe the man had a dog, maybe not.
Then, on a straight stretch, the weather comes down.

Snow on a peak lifts and spins in the cloud.
Mass is suspended, the hillsides withdraw.
Valleys returning beneath us blank out.
When we have left them or if we come back
mountains go nowhere. They sit there all year.

We were both thinking and watching the road.
I didn't mention the person on foot.
Somewhere back then maybe, sometime out there
two sketchy figures have come to the ridge.
One doesn't stop but treks on through the air
searching for something and lost in himself.

Ynyslas

The night was banging on the walls
the neighbouring house or two
had turned away and shut.

Beyond the reading light, the streets
across the estuary
were lit in another county

and the train that went through
was an hour or so before.
Otherwise there was just the book.

You would have felt the mile-long breakers
up through the soles of your feet
if you had been out there on the sands.

In the morning there was
the littered beach, the sunken forest
and the bells from last night's pages.

Now, a whole life on, the night
sometimes shakes the walls
and underwater bells start swinging.

A bird's foot from Jack

The doorway is a bar of shrinking gold. It goes to nothing, clicks
shut. You turn the key, pull down your hat. Only the blood-red
streetlights punctuate the night as you head up the hill, when Jack
at number nine pops out in his work clothes. He hands you
a bird's foot telling you it might come in handy, then goes back in
saying those floorboards won't lift themselves.

You duck along hedges and over the playing fields, come
to a stretch of dual-carriageway between a field of carrots and
a business park. The pages there have gold edging and scuffed
green leather bindings, paw pads and signs of hasty gorgings
have overwritten themselves repeatedly in the muddy verges
and there's a danger that your name will get lost among them.

You bed down in traffic-din by a torn water course among
brambles, wind-ripped plastic sheeting, and tell yourself how
these are times of collision, write with the bird's foot how culverts
and sub-stations are being held hard against the Chancellor's men
in long goblin wars that must continue because he sold all
the silver and children but still can't pay off the interest.

In your bits and pieces of coat you shift out of town towards
morning where children and birds once sang in your head as well
as in the trees. You wonder when it was that the doors got shut on
the perpetual hills as if they had just been books going back on the
shelves in a library some closing time. But it comes as no surprise
to find your old house has become a department store.

You recognise the stairs but not a lot seems familiar among the floors of purchasable items. Going up, the echo sounds the same as you listen for voices you would know. And the corridor that this time takes you through soft furnishings was always there, the passage through rock, the track through mountains towards friends, the unlit path, the road to the water's edge.

Late evening. The reed beds are silent. There's a crunching of footfall on the causeway ahead, but the shape just in front of you in the hat is simply your shadow. Although your name is a fading imprint of claws you can still touch the silt and the surface, or ask yourself what Jack, lit blood-red, was doing under his floorboards. There are no stars just unpronounceable blue.

Travelling through the amapolas
'To think is to see with eyes that are unwell.'
Alberto Caeiro, 8 March 1914, trans. Richard Zenith

The sky is now something quite different
there are enormous plants like nothing at all
and when you signal your wishes
you receive in reply only imaginary gifts
because during this translation
you have become absent from words
that once came as easily as water.

I could say these are mountains
but we're not going to the mountains
that behind white walls on a hill there's a park
or is it a cemetery? I could point out
we're passing through somewhere they call
Two Sisters, but I don't know the story
any more than I can tell you whose horse that is.

And if I don't make any proper apology
for such shaky interpretations
(if it turns out the horse was a mule)
that hawk of some kind hanging up there
has no names I suppose in its head at all
yet it sees the small things hiding
in what for now I'll call grass.

Don't think though I mean to be unfriendly.
I can still tell you for certain the flowers
alongside the track are amapolas, and these
swimming among the bridges are swifts.
Later together we'll watch bats
whispering through the pillars of Hercules
high among trees we don't know.

Steps

i.m. Ruth Stone

She was a teacher too, might well
have given a swifter answer
if asked, as I was by my student
what it was I had learned from them.

That teaching and learning is a bridge
where we meet halfway then walk together
to a place that I'm familiar with
I replied, though some time later.

Years later still I ask myself
who was crossing which way why
and if in fact we were the bridge
rather than foot traffic over it.

As a teacher too she might have said
give them this to consider: the girders
of the bridge are air that lets us step
with unsteady words across a river.

1400m from Silver Street
after Richard Long, A Walk in Avon – 1986

Count steps to Bridewell Street down Nelson Street
feeling the footpath vibrating. We ask
our phones or ourselves *is this where we are?*
400 metres, outside Blue Arrow.

At the end of Quay Street there is no quay
among the fountains no trams, as we walk
through time, the bombing raids, or by tall ships
where ferries leave from the hidden river.

You turn left into Queen Square. Plane trees ssh
above lunchtime, gulls, William III.
At Welsh Back, Avon Fire and Rescue drive
slow, flame red, over the floating harbour

and beyond the lights St Mary Redcliffe
points a gold bird at the one o'clock sun.

Man and beast

Top man he kept calling me in Licata's
> *'separating man from beast*
> *since 1986'*
> where I got a number one all over.

It was Heart or Jack FM they had on
> as he gestured me towards
> a chunky padded chair
> with splits in the leatherette.

Number one then, he said, tying
> the off-white nylon tight
> round my neck before slotting
> a number one into his clippers.

There's always the jumble of leads, attachments
> scissors, tissues, branded preparations
> repeated in the row of mirrors
> on the tatty toffee-coloured shelf.

There's always the big soft brush after the razor
> down the back of the neck
> powdery and greasy at the same time
> as tiny hairs fly in the perfumed air.

He presented my head in the hand-mirror
> we agreed, then he undid the drape
> let down the chair and called me top man
> one more time when I paid at the counter.

Even smelling of cologne going along
> Filton Avenue by the shut chip shop
> and Bargain Booze, you feel
> number one all over some days.

Nightfall on Broadquay

The centre is not The Centre, nor Broadmead or Bristol Bridge.
We can get to these on buses, but not so the true centre.

We could search for it together, where the plane trees branch
beneath asphalt thunder and its shaking of the red-mud night

where residues and slops will be muddled and mislabelled
by the upside-down curators of our imaginations

who then place in our path such calcinated clams and eels
as clog disconnected pipes and colour-coded cabling.

We might sleepwalk by abandoned gratings there, rotted wharfage
iron gates that never open, lost slipways and dead-end steps.

How would we be woken though, how would we get back again?
Maybe we would come up in springtime like some Jesus flower

or rise inside the hairs of trees, if slowly, by osmosis
where afloat on blood, the slave ships offloaded mostly sugar

where this century's gulls, fixed-winged kites, white as holy ghosts
turn between the only windows that can reach the last of day.

Yet in the end I'm not sure we'll find it on the harbour
which is not the centre either. Could it be these drinkers though

these diners in their flowered shirts their shoes like knives, if not
the beggars of the past and present, the crews of sunken ships?

Or it could be how the city lights reflect on stone on skin
and on all its fabrics equally, could be this nightfall now.

A470

Behind you is the church
visible from everywhere
the girlfriend still at school
brothers and sisters, your parents
sheepish on the concrete forecourt
as the bus is pulling out
and last the ring of hills.

The road before you vanishes
towards Philosophy
or whatever learning
lies beyond a mountain.

Today you are not sure
how much you ever left behind
but your memory kept for reference
the little you will need
      the hills
      the bus
      the road.

JET TRAILS

Pink moon
22 June 2016

Most the long day bent the grass
and nettles, poured wet threads
through handfuls of unripe fruit
then cleared by early evening,
wide above us like a flag opening,
filled with the scales and skin
of a cloudy fish come slowly in,
its eye a pink moon rising through
dark blue leaves and shining smoke.

I took pictures on my phone
while maps and monsters flowed
from half-lit room to room.
But next day all I'd have
was questions such as why a fish
that size had left no traces.

Our cities buzzed and flashed below
as if these conjunctions could come again
or a nation could not slip its mooring
nightmares couldn't be there in the morning
dressing in our clothes to go and claim
that nothing much need ever change

which tomorrow's length of day disproves
likewise the absence now of nightingales
the present darkness of the moon.

From nowhere

'If you believe you are a citizen of the world
you are a citizen of nowhere.'
Theresa May PM, 8 March 2016

We are here on an apple on a tree in deep space
or on some other kind of fruit or planet
in the middle of what we call October.

In this October at a time called afternoon
the leaves of climbing beans are turning yellow
their green machinery slowing as the light goes.

Sun drains from them, and bright sugars
are left behind to crystallise. The stalks
of sweetcorn peas sweetpeas beans go tough.

Citizens of this month or other world
they rustle and rattle now where they hang
among a few improbable flowers

and leaves have already started falling
the means of their production slowing,
this October afternoon time on this planet.

As these last round days tip towards a winter
and long times in the republic of nowhere
curling documents are crumbling underfoot.

Jet trails
after Stanley Kunitz from Alexander Blok

Streetlight, roofline, jet trail, plane.
All day the news has not been good.
You know this so I won't explain
and I'm not confident I could.

Sometimes the atmosphere confirms
that love and colour are the same.
The stars are drowned, the sun returns.
Streetlight, roofline, jet trail, plane.

A photograph of Rilke

'Lay your shadow now on the sundials,'
Rainer Maria Rilke, October Day, trans. Robert Bly

It is the light of winter coming
he has stepped into, right hand holding
at shoulder height the edge of the archway
where he emerges onto a balcony.

It is the long ago of off-white paper
a blankness representing passing day
a printed moment in that late October
falling in strips through a plain balustrade.

His creased trousers, tight collar, his skin
are rendered equal by the afternoon.
Tie, neat hair, trees nearly bare behind him.
Rilke, eyes as dark as the arch, half turns.

And if we can't know what he sees, he looks
towards us as though himself unsure
what shadows might be leaning through that hour
might be translated on the pages of a book.

Early Hepworth

A tree with no green
or bark. Finely cut
the cured hardwood goes
up oil-shiny
and dark from the base.

Decapitated
lopped at the shoulders
slight moon breasts, belly
that does not slacken
knees that do not give

but this woman tree
twists at the pelvis
a little, the back
turns along the grain

if solid, is full
of the half-hidden
summers and winters
the swelling circles
that surface as skin.

An alarm protects
this statue. So touch
and the bees will come
Artemis or Pan
will chop you down here.

Battle of Britain
After the 2017 tapestry of the same name by Grayson Perry

In the army you spent months in a tent, then you pitched this one
under the M20. You keep your kit tidy, but get pinned down
by rifle fire in Afghanistan every time the volume of traffic hits
a certain level.

It must seem a different picture on the other side of the railway.
They don't know you were one of Our Boys, and their terrace
of blank gardens, motor home, the St George's Cross, looks
as dismal as any tent city.

So imagine it's all some kind of carpet hung on a long white wall,
people coming to look saying nothing or 'That's just how it is.'
Imagine I wave, we shake hands, I step in you step out. There I go
and here you are.

While I mooch off towards your fire, you pick up where I left off
gazing across the edges of England – the tracks, dual carriageways
hedges pylons turbines diminishing towards the clouds the coast
even Dunkirk or Calais.

I listen to rumbling concrete at the graffitied foot of your pier
think about a friend who lost his mind, lend a lighter to someone
who starts cooking up. Funny what bubbles and spits in the spoon
came from Afghanistan.

You walk away in my coat and shoes down the gallery stairs to sit
in a café I know. You see people who aren't there, a gun goes
fuckfuckfuck your friend trips a switch there's blood-brains-bone.
Your coffee arrives.

Later, the lights in town will be nightfire. Till then your mates
are still dead, mine's gone mad, there's art in the sky, the park's
full of crackheads. *Everything you could want in a pantomime.*
We stare at our walls.

Both in and out, lit up printed or sprayed, they tell truths of a kind
   Go all out on iPhone X Smak Buzz R.I.P.
    Aladdin at The Hippodrome
    Vote Leave Toffs Out Class War

'Who would I be when I listened to a piece of music?'
Frank Serpico in conversation with actor Al Pacino

I could be walking along a previous century to talk
to the citizens of its walls and to look through their windows.

I could be at their tables of trompe l'oeil fruit and knives of oil
or a meal that ends in crumbs of light and beads of blood-red wine

but their lips would stay shut, their eyes flat on the canvas,
and the light of the past in the harbour would only be gold.

Or I could be sitting at the doors of my ears and waiting
for a pianist to run up a staircase of keys

but the nocturne would come dull as hammers on scaffold boards
its nominal moon ringing flat as a coin on a pavement.

Then I would be lying awake, doors open or doors locked tight
and there would be no point at all, no soundless bell.

In the morning colour would fail or cloud would only be cloud
and the rain would not land like jumping fish in the pools it made

because I had not stood, because I had not given or had not said
because I walked past, my hands in my pockets, eyes to the ground

I suppose I stood, I suppose I gave, was not always mute
and surely I only walked by when my pockets were empty.

So who am I when the omissions start to amount to one weight
when these scales and refractions are tumbling around in the night?

Who am I anyway rising and falling, adrift in this,
names and pieces of music bubbling up then fading out?

Who am I wakeful and alone in the night with my breathing
with what's done, not done or undone, and what's left behind?

Number eleven

And here we are a few feet from the door
that I have now no right to take you through.
And I have not stood here like this before
or if I have, not side by side with you.

The door is closed. There were no other ways
the burning of this season has begun.
There are no other years, no plural days.
This late September is the only one.

This afternoon the door is glossy black
though I remember it as shabby green.
A child on the other side is back
who will not see himself and can't be seen.

Those days, today, and one day stand and fall.
The rain came in – I think I said before.
I am a child, am not a child at all
and now there is no going through the door.

Home truths 1963

Our father was not made of money jam or butter.
Our mother seemed not made of anything.
We must give thanks for butter
and all the things of which our father is not made.

If there's a man in a suit my parents aren't at home.
If it's the phone we will see first if our parents are in.
To certain people they are most definitely out.
Backward sloping writing means a dishonest nature.

Life is a constant series of disappointments.
It is the hereafter in which we put our trust.
There is no need to have it all when one can settle for less.
There is always tomorrow, though tomorrow never comes.

One must at all times not slouch but sit straight.
When walking one should pick one's feet up.
Above all one should speak truthfully and properly.
I will go bald if I don't learn to waggle my ears.

It is evening in April or in October.
The hereafter comes floating through the trees
spreads itself across the tea-time table.
Having eaten everything and said grace we may get down.

Creases

A sort of night has fallen on my hands
a length of days is darkening the skin
has made them flecked estuarial hinterlands.
The veins are thick, their ground is parchment thin.
What they have held has made familiar marks
left livid tracks, as have the moons and suns
that ring the various contracts of the heart
and hold the promises till flesh is done.

They make an offer if I open them,
become a question in an empty book.
I could be shackled here, could be condemned
or showing you the only place to look
which in the end is all they can release
the shining and the shadow of each crease.

House with its head in its hands

In a city that had ships in its heart
this house imagines itself on a shore
pictures the sky in its windows passing
over the street and the neighbouring streets.

As every house has its head in its hands
sometimes, so this one up late this winter
is listening to the night in the chimney
can hear it coming in under the door.

And I find myself here asking myself
why it is I try to heal the walls
and spend all this time on fixing the heart
while the house is sailing through the winter.

So this house holding its head in its hands,
now imagines itself in a harbour,
is listening to the silence, or the wind,
which is the same thing, hissing like a tide.

The wardrobe mirror

Some days you wear the season's weather
        its cloud formations, its cloths of rain
you put on the upper atmosphere
        its goose striations, textures of wren.

Sometimes I watch you become the sea.
        Opening the door of the wardrobe
you pull out curled weeds pools blue-greens
        you hang the foreshore from your earlobes.

There are evenings when you take your time
        fix a column of jet to each ear
and Venus low in the south west shines
        out of the folds of your hems of air.

Sometimes you are clothed in a field.
        I lie there too, awake in the dark
counting the flowers or looking for keys
        while you sleep in the intertwined plants.

Someday, dressed in wood, we'll come undone
        be loosened in subsoil or fire
then put all the seasons' colours on
        all the oceans, as we did before.

THE LADIES AND GENTLEMEN OF THE DEAD

Hardware visitations
after Allen Ginsberg, A Supermarket in California

I found I was fragile under the apple blossom
this crystal blue spring, so I took myself off down the hill
to get brackets and fixings.

Ginsberg, I thought of you on the way
though couldn't put my finger on why, considered whether
it was solitude or some sense my nation was losing its mind.

I confess I felt I needed some ticket or token
some pass to eternity to open a gate
or a sliding glass door of admission to Eden.

But you know how it is
though they promise a kingdom the prophets stay dead
the lamb that is slaughtered gets eaten and the galaxies never reply

and like anyone else with a diary
that keeps filling with funerals, I had a shelf to put up on a wall
and I needed some hardware.

As I arrived with my list the store was busy as usual,
the entrance was crowded with buckets and brushes
like offerings to sensible gods.

And I saw you there, Allen Ginsberg,
wistful among doorknobs and latch sets feeling
the smoothness of finger plates and eyeing a helpful assistant.

You were there too, Lieutenant Wilfred Owen
in your bloodied uniform browsing the padlocks
the hooks and turn buttons in labelled trays.

I saw you step back politely as someone was shown
where tool clips were. Did these bits and pieces
remind you of home, or your kit in the trenches?

You who fought having written that the sweetness of death
by war was a lie, and you who blew dope smoke
in the face of war, I wanted to introduce you.

In my mind I said, will we carry on down together
and get some fish, take it back to my place
to have with white wine under a flowering tree?

Where this all started in fact. Wilfred, will you recount
how your housemaster quoted Horace, then nodding knowingly
sauntered off to watch cricket?

Will you recount for us, Allen,
your rhapsodic nights on benzedrine, or explain in cogent detail
why America must impeach her president?

I may not get to these verses before
you board the ferry together laughing and shouting
that *dulce et decorum est, pro patria mori.*

As you step unsteadily on the smoking shore
will you pay the oarsman in mirror plates, picture hooks
buttons and other little bits of brass?

Lunch with Borges

'I'm not sure I exist, actually.' Jorge Luis Borges

A friend of mine is having lunch this afternoon
with Jorge Francisco Isidoro Luis Borges
whose birthday it is today.

It's an odd relationship, but Borges
the much older man (if such comparisons now apply)
has taken my friend on as a kind of protégé.

Both are students of philosophy, Borges albeit
as an existential paradoxical fabulist
while my friend is mainly a logical positivist.

Both are linguists who speak each other's mother tongue
though I imagine Borges will insist on English
with amusing sorties into several Latin languages.

It should make for an interesting lunch, long and boozy.
I can just hear my friend posing ontological questions
as Borges wryly offers him the last purple langoustine.

By the time they get to dessert I expect I'll be home
and already chopping things up for a curry tonight
while they linger over a last glass of late harvest Malbec.

I don't know what Borges would make of curry.
Not much I suspect. My friend would concede
that Shakespeare had little to say on the subject.

The waiters will of course be angelic
will like as not join in with Persian ghazals
and then help the pair into their unnecessary overcoats.

So where will they go after lunch as I'm dicing aubergines?
I imagine my friend will take them up in his aeroplane
both of them chuckling over the ironies.

Jorge Luis Borges turned 107 today,
my friend the pilot is arguably 61.
It makes no odds now both of them are dead.

Avenue Principal
Cimetière du Père-Lachaise, for CRL

This is a suburb, leafy, quiet, and if not
for the communards and déportés, it is well-to-do.

Bonjour, and how are you today Madame?
Thank you Monsieur, still dead, and yourself?

Still dead too Madame, tired of listening to insects.
Quite so, and rain trickling in at one's ears.

The sound of trees drinking what is left of us.
Drinking and drinking, taller and taller.

They fade away together on the Avenue Principal
among sepulchres like narrow houses.

The grilles for front doors incorporate
crosses, roses, here and there a star.

Blackbirds blacker than marble monuments
eat the richest worms in Paris, sing

in green and yellow chestnut leaves
above Famille Forel, Famille Defourmental-Latierre

above Marie Elise Toussaint de Quiévrecourt
Famille Blanc, Famille Espace, Famille Éclipsé.

Madame, I regret I do not recall who you might be.
Nor I, nor why roots have tied us up together here.

Nightfall now. Sabotine, Boucher, Charpentier, Pecheur
and comrades are cuffed and cussed and dragged along.

No blackbirds sing tonight, Messieurs, and we suppose
the ironies are not lost on you

of your summary execution against the wall
of this furthest corner of a cemetery

where a Himalayan tree holds cones of flowers
in darkness in its many hundred hands

where a weight of letters was later lifted up
Dachau   Auschwitz   Bergen-Belsen   Buchenwald

Could you eat a roasted blackbird, or just its tongue?
  No my dear, no thank you, not just now.

A little wine though might be good, red wine like blood.
  Yes, I remember. Something to enrich the rain.

So whose are those stone children, ours perhaps?
And what is this whispering of names, addresses?

It is a dissolution of what we were
the words we are, what we do not know.

It is our slowly turning into trees.

The ladies and gentlemen of the dead

Sometimes these skeletons are down on their kneecaps
                praying for wings
                to a bone moon
although there is only shadow, night air
                and no breath
                between their ribs.
Through the holes on either side above their jaws they hear
                or do not hear
                the roaring void.
They frown at black-winged hourglasses, turn
                sockets towards
                the streams of sand
the grains of which are diamonds crowns and wheels
                of silicone
                and calcium.
Gnawing at the leftovers of themselves
                in churchyards
                and charnel grounds
these ladies and gentlemen of the dead are
                white as sugar
                bright as salt.
Their digits rustle your keyboard, your devices
                your pages
                your wardrobe.
They climb allegorical trees, turn up
                as escutcheons
                and silver rings
gurn from gallery walls, become tattoos
                grin from clocks
                and graffitti.
Look how they salute the generals that a president
                puts on parade
                then executes

how their empty pates become instructive cups
                for dope smokers
                and anchorites.
Yet in the end these puppets are brittle and hollow
                with one cracked tune
                one febrile dance
as they batter at side-drums, grip flat bagpipes
                or thigh-bone flutes
                between their teeth.
So then at the first bird or bell, or when one star
                burns on the hills
                in a green dawn
the rattling stops and the boxes cupboards and coffins
                are closed again.

Coming in to Holy Island

Italic names are vessels assisted by Holy Island lifeboats

I told the seals lolling on their haul-outs
how I'd blown in once again, insomniac
down braided channels, over sandbanks,
the shallows of the causeway and across
its tracts of doubtful land.

Breadwinner of Holy Island
Provider of Holy Island

I'm half-wrecked in the wheelhouse, I said,
I'm a flare in a gale, a fishing boat in sealight
flying on the tide. Guide me to the harbour,
beach me in the marram grass, in the godspell
of its sound of sand.

Fingal of Dublin   Ellen Fairburn of Eyemouth
Gustav Vigeland of Bergen

And I will be an owl tacking through the dark,
quartering the field, scanning for a movement,
or I'll be the signal lighting up the phones,
making pagers bleep, fading out or surging
on VHF on Holy Island.

Jupiter of Liverpool   Lizzie of Fowey
Mischief of Carnarvon   Rumleigh of Aberdeen

I'll become the vision that a famished hermit
has of flying dragons at high tide on his rock,
I'll be his distant seal-cry Pater Noster
or the oystercatcher's calling from the saltmarsh
and leave no trace on land.

SS Helmsdale of Ipswich   SS Darlington of Stockholm
Sloop Elizabeth of Sunderland

I made my promises to mussel-crusted outcrops
to curling blue-grey water, water pale as flatfish
silver as a herring, whistling black or fogbound
or sucking at the run-off streaming from
beaches on the mainland.

   Annie Stewart of Banff Edith Cavell of Seahouses
    Sailor Prince of North Shields

I'll be gone again by morning, and leave
no more record on the mudflats than a wader
no more signs than a curlew in the dunes, I said.

    Eventide of Holy Island
    Guiding Star of Holy Island

Sleepless on the dog-watch we went down
finding sleep at last, or came upon salvation
in the rocking of the lifeboat, on the monk roads
of illuminated strands.

    Bring us home to Holy Island
    Eventide and Guiding Star
     of Holy Island

Number 1A
Jackson Pollock, 1948

Colour has its hurricanes, light its own tides, though we're here too
somewhere. How else would we know the calm that comes at last
here where things jitterbug just out of sight of the tracks they leave
when you get smashed? Wrench the cropped bone open and tip
whiskey in, spew it forth as shredded flags, unrecorded storms
as busted nests of nerves or thorn tongues that sing nothing at all
in the booze-banged brain's knife-fight on the floor with white.
Because it's coming, the Oldsmobile smash one mile from home.
Yet these feathers, flat distances, unspooling bales of fence wire
these black lightnings in hailstone-packed scrub, this petal-dabbed
impasto sheet of jazz, and this summoning of both bad juju and
earthly delights is paint with no centre. Big seas roll on, but blood
flick-flecked in surf clinches it anyway. So he flew up fifty feet
into that birch tree, ended red-scribble dead bird there in fifty-six.

Black star
*i.m. David Bowie ***

The first day one summer
a soot crystal
dark snowflake or flower
is falling through white space.

It goes below the lines
through the gateway of itself
into border zones
of other information

drifts down from visible
towards invisible
where creatures light themselves
settles on the sea bed.

**I'm not a white star
I'm a black star*

It is night at altitude
we are stone blind
among blizzards of asterisks.

Losing ourselves on the page
we become dark flowers
in white space.

It is the first day one summer.

Pictures of us that I haven't got

Here are some pictures of us, Rob,
that I haven't got. They don't rhyme much either
what with things being tough enough right now.

The first is us drinking your girlfriend's Pernod
all of it, while she sleeps upstairs and we talk
to the sound of the sea sweeping Borth beach clean.

Lots more from then, a bit blurred. I like this one
in the back of a Land Rover off to a party
all baa-ing like sheep in case the police see us.

Bit of a theme here. A session at Ocean Wave.
You and the girl you picked up have just nicked
my girlfriend's bed as we're going up on acid.

The ones of Wales are all funny colours now
but the ones from London on our training course
where you met your first wife are a bit sharper.

I think I was supposed to get off with her friend.
Sylvia was her name, but I was too absorbed
in the present perfect continuous and so forth.

You're not in this one. Me and Nigel in Turkey.
Some desolate disco with the gin looking weird
in the lights, snow and gunfire out in the night.

Barcelona was more fun. More fish. In this one
an octopus is coming out of the wall
huge, pink, steaming, and whole from the cooker.

In this bar they did pig's ears and cider.
Remember how Nigel got pickpocketed once
had to sneak back on the train with no ticket?

Here I've walked through a glass door in the small hours
at the bottom of the stairs. I've still got a scar
and I had to give you some money to get home with.

It's amazing our wives married us really.
I guess we kind of settled down.
I guess there was a wildness we never forgot.

This picture that I haven't actually got
is the last, though we didn't know it then.
London briefly, Nigel's gone home on his train.

A cold December evening, as it is now
a pub boat lit up and moored on the north bank.
On deck, wine and a spliff for you, beer for me.

I'm in my best hat and coat looking, you said,
like a Hungarian spy. You're in jacket and jeans
and we're talking about children and business.

I haven't got one of you in the chemical sunshine
where you presently are. I hope it's strong.
I hope they've given you the really good stuff.

As the river goes past us into the dark, it's time
to drink up. See, there we are, stepping off the boat.
                    Adéu.

Osip Mandelstam's boat

'Who can know from the word goodbye
What kind of parting is in store for us?'
Osip Mandelstam, Tristia, trans. Richard Greene

I knew this green-brown river wasn't the Neva.
I knew a city in the south-west of England
could not be Petrograd or St Petersburg.
But for the course of this afternoon's return
I had decided it could at least be Leningrad
and it was no surprise at Bennett Street to see you
at a door where the porch was a curving shell
full as a sail, trim as verses crossing classical times
and the black sea, Osip, of your own exiles.

We walked down to greyed limestone parapets.
They were warm to the touch as we watched
gulls below us dipping on and off the water.
I pointed out for you which way the coast lay
turned to say 'But let me show you over there
the haberdashery, pies, and second-hand books
where just beyond the entrance we might hear
my father arguing with a butcher, then touch
and all but taste costume jewellery, or buy tea.'

This was how, in the market's cool dark, we were
just in time to see my younger self with a friend.
We followed, but lost them in the guitar shop
as they went a back way past pianos to racks
of records A to Z that they could not afford.
Then I find I'm not sure what year this is exactly.
I know there was no violet shadow on snowfall
on the towpath as we exchanged carefully folded
sheets of paper by an iron bridge over the canal.

We shook hands at the station, and although
I could still imagine you at a bay window there
looking out across sloping terraces, Nadezhda
writing at a card table behind you, I didn't expect
us to meet again, either in my old home town
or here where I've lived undisturbed for years.
So turning a page in a second-hand bookshop
it took me some time to realise that it was you
crossing that brittle yellow twilight in a boat.

The names

The dead are sitting there on the benches in pairs
and in singles staring out over the North Sea
the Atlantic, the Irish Sea or the Channel.
There are bluebells, mustards, violets in the hollows.

Behind them time has spattered the wall with lichen
the wind has clipped the hawthorn and tamped it down tight.
When you pass them on the dusty clifftop footpath
they pull back their feet as they wish you good morning.

They are fixed there in an endless two-week summer
a bank-holiday weekend lasting for ever
to hardwood, to durable recycled plastic.
Margaret and John, Mum and Dad, Maureen, Robert, George.

This is what we worked hard for. This is where we came
even times when the weather was disappointing
where the skylarks still climb up and down their own songs
and where there are flowers we don't know the names of.

We were not rich, we did our best, we had some laughs
we got to know others, and now we all sit here
among gorse bushes yellower than the sunshine
watching ships as they slide along the horizon.

The nameplates face the early sun, the evening sun
a headland, a town in the bay. Their drumless ears
kept wakeful by gulls are hushed by the tides. Their mouths
empty of life are tasting the salt on the wind.

You stand slightly sideways on the horns of the moon

You look down slightly sideways
placidly on us saying nothing
as we pester you with names

        Mother of   Sorrows
                    Mercy
                    the Poor
        Queen of Heaven
        Star of the Sea
        Our Lady of the Pillar
                the Hill
                the Mountain
                the Snows
                the Thorn

for help with the troublesome business
of getting answers from a male abstraction

Some days you flicker in flowers bare feet
on a snake or the horns of the moon
and we weep wax and wine
while a man in a hat like a spaceship
carefully invokes all our mothers

Your legal position as Mother of God
is fiendish and the whole deal
has always been complicated
        Yet you stand to one side
of all the gold altars to your son
albeit in looted silver
        like a suitcase in the lobby
or rise through the rays of heaven
divested of grief and fertility
        in acres of fabric

In many respects you left
        with no luggage
missing out the departure lounge
        completely
blue and white into blue and white
        then a flare of silver
slightly sideways I think
        saying nothing

Dark Albion

Suppose there was a darker Albion
beneath us, thick as porter, fat as eels
a flag of anthracite blood-crossed and torn
a country where we might be stiffed by deals
that got signed off while we were still asleep
or selling sandwiches for bugger all
making ghost calls from half a mile deep
hauling nets or ploughing sooty fields.
So who might rule in that unpleasant land
or chair the grisly boards who rigged the rules
to push that mouldered Blighty's tainted brand?
The splendid chaps, no doubt, who always do,
venturers who shipped half-dead flesh for gold
or mined the nation's sparking crown of coal.

Who dug then for the nation's crown of coal
or trawled its seas for silver coins by night?
Fools like us, skipper, bringing up the shoals
hand over hand raw blue with salt and ice.
And then what hearts of oak sailed full-rigged ships
with pots and pans along the Guinea coast?
Us again, with your shackles ropes and whips
and we're still out there fishing for our souls.
Such things we did at sea we'll never tell
while other things we never saw we'll say.
We're tacking in against a wind from hell
that blows our prayers away in any case.
Look, swinging there, the harbour lights ahead,
or else the lights of islands of the dead.

And if this is an island of the dead
we're buried women stitching up its seams
picking coals pressing trousers tying threads
shifting shitty stains lining up machines.
Or sewing letters on the linen air
above the garden of some lovely home
and picturing fine gentry living there
our Master and our Mistress when we're grown.
But if this is an island of the blind
then you won't know us when you wash up here
while we do your dirty work, sharing eyes
exchanging teeth and needles, tongues and ears.
We'll know your names, we'll see and hear you though
down in the sculleries among the bones.

Come with us through the sculleries and bones
through grits and gravels into heavy clay
below tin tabernacles and priest holes
across the surfaces of unlit lakes
where giant woodlice left their tracks on stone
where oceans laid their fathom loads of shell.
Come through the granites and conglomerates
gneisses, marls, schists, the basalts and shales.
And we will reach the banks of streams of fire
but meet no lost friends or whispering souls.
The rebel angels didn't fall this far.
There's nothing and no one except ourselves
a thousand miles underneath the rain
or a harvest moon on Albion's lanes.

A harvest moon rolls down Albion's lanes
and in a dream you had between two wars.
Its shadow hands among the stacks of hay
track through stubble and over drystone walls.
There are moths on nettles, eyes in the thorns
as that fat moon lights a wood on the hills.
Maybe a dog barks on a distant farm
but otherwise the ink-blue air is still.
Or another moon hangs in later stars
like a flag of pure electricity
that crackles over town, shines on the stairs
arches through the night across a city.
This cold obverse or same moon sails on
till a gold dawn breaks over Albion.

No golden dawn so far in Albion
where it's as En-ger-land as HP Sauce
a lion rampant and a unicorn
a nil-nil draw then sweet and sour pork.
Right now prospects look as black as pudding
Whitby jet and masochistic leather
oil on a beach, the Downing Street railings
horses nodding plumes of funeral feathers.
The relatives are squabbling at a wake
among the teacups crisps and sausages
or are determining affairs of state
while clutching fizz and little sandwiches.
How sick will we feel by bleary dawn
then all through the bright hungover morning?

The air is thin, cold but clear this morning.
The north side of our street is briefly gold
even while last night goes on muttering
'You built Jerusalem but now it's sold.'
Heavy traffic is heading into town,
an ordinary working week has begun.
So we stand at the bus stop, check our phones
and stare into space until the bus comes.
It wasn't us who crewed the slavers' ships
or cast ourselves adrift from the mainland.
We've got a job to get to, or the shops
on a late winter's weekday in England.
The front door's locked, last night's black dreams are done.
Suppose though that this was Dark Albion.

Faded out

A Constable print is what you'd expect.
It goes with the brown of the bannisters
and the busy pattern in the carpet
but I hardly notice it as we pass
remembering out loud the way to his room.

Constable was a favourite, but today
a thick sleep has fallen on my father
has silenced what he might have imparted
about the application of oils
to represent the English countryside.

That's where he was most at home, in a time
of apparent unchanging certitude
which I see in the print as we're leaving
though its colours have all but faded out
and as you said, there's nothing left but blue.

A line of black shoes

Three pairs of polished black shoes on the floor
his daughter-in-law's, his grandson's, and mine.

Polishing shoes was how we used to spend
the last of Sunday before prayers and bed.

'I want to see my face in them,' he'd say.
Perhaps that meant something during the war.

He was flanked by six candles in the end.
I sang the hymns and heard him in my head.

I made a good job of the shoes that day
and of course I saw his face in the shine.